Step-by-Step
Handmade Cards

Tamsin Carter

Heinemann Library
Chicago, Illinois

© 2002 Reed Educational & Professional Publishing
Published by Heinemann Library,
an imprint of Reed Educational & Professional Publishing,
Chicago, Illinois

Customer Service 888-454-2279

Visit our website at www.heinemannlibrary.com

Photographs by Charlotte de la Bédoyère, Search Press Studios
Photographs and design copyright © Search Press Limited, 2002

Text copyright © Tamsin Carter 2002
Designed by Search Press
Printed in Italy by L.E.G.O.

06 05 04 03 02
10 9 8 7 6 5 4 3 2 1

Library of Congress Cataloging-in-Publication Data

Carter, Tamsin.
    Handmade cards / Tamsin Carter.
        p. cm. -- (Step-by-step)
    Includes index.
    ISBN 1-40340-698-7 (HC),   1-40340-717-0 (Pbk)
      1. Greeting cards--Juvenile literature. [1. Greeting cards.
2. Handicraft.] I. Title. II. Step-by-step (Heinemann Library)
    TT872.T35 2002
    745. 594'1--dc21

                                                2001059373

Acknowledgments
The author and publishers are grateful to the following for
permission to reproduce copyright material:
Mary Evans Picture Library, page 5.

Photographs: Search Press Studios

Every effort has been made to contact copyright holders of any
material reproduced in this book. Any omissions will be rectified in
subsequent printings if notice is given to the publisher.

This book is dedicated to Steve Carter,
who makes life better than I
ever dreamed.

Some words are shown in bold, **like this.**
You can find out what they mean by
looking in the glossary.

When this sign is used in the
book, it means that adult
supervision is needed.

REMEMBER!
Ask an adult to help you
when you see this sign.

Contents

Introduction

Commercial greeting cards are sent for all sorts of reasons: to wish someone a happy birthday or good luck; to celebrate a holiday, such as Christmas or New Years; to say thank you, congratulations, or just hello. A greeting card tells someone that you are thinking of him or her and that you care, and it gives the person a picture to display. Just think how much more special a handmade card is because you have created it yourself and chosen the message personally.

People all over the world have been sending each other hand-decorated messages and cards for hundreds of years, probably since paper became widely available. The oldest known Valentine's card was made in the 1400s and is now in the British Museum in London, England. Printed cards came later, in the nineteenth century, and were mainly for celebrating holidays or religious festivals.

In this book you will learn how to make a variety of cards using a range of materials including felt, pipe cleaners, beads, and even wobbly plastic eyes! Do not worry if you think you cannot draw very well—there are patterns in the back of the book to help you. There is also a section on page 28 that shows you easy methods of **transferring** designs and **scoring** and folding posterboard. There are lots of fun techniques to try, such as paint spattering, sewing, and collage.

Inspiration can come from all sorts of sources. If you think of the person you are making the card for, that may get you started. In this book there are cards inspired by space, nature, musical instruments, dinosaurs, sports, famous artists, and ancient wonders. Once you have chosen your subject, you can investigate it further by searching for information in libraries, galleries, museums, and on the Internet.

Nature is a very good place to find inspiration. You can collect leaves, sticks, and flowers to make a collage, or look at the weather and the amazing effects it has on our world. Sometimes the materials themselves can be inspiring: just laying them out in front of you can be enough to trigger an idea and get you started.

Most importantly remember there are no rules—the more you experiment and dare to try something new, the more wonderful your cards will be. A card can be simple or complicated. It can take an hour to make or just five minutes. A greeting card is very special, it is a gift and a message all in one. Enjoy making these cards, and people will enjoy receiving them.

*Greeting cards first became popular in **Victorian** times. This beautifully painted nineteenth-century Christmas card shows the ornate and detailed style typical of the Victorians.*

Materials

The items pictured here are the basic materials that you will need to make the projects in this book. Cards are not expensive to make and you can find a lot of the items shown here at home. Start collecting pieces of colored paper and cardboard, string and ribbons, beads, buttons, pictures from magazines, and even old greeting cards. You can cut these up and recycle them to create your own original designs. Soon you will have a box of treasures to dip into whenever you are feeling creative.

Colored *pipe cleaners* are great fun and can be bent into almost any shape.

Note Remember to cover your work surface with newspaper or scrap paper before using paints or glue.

Pencils are used for drawing and to **transfer** designs. A *ballpoint pen* that has run out of ink is used to **score** cardboard. A *compass* is used to draw circles and to pierce holes.

A clear *sandwich bag* is used to create a window for the Winter Window card on page 26.

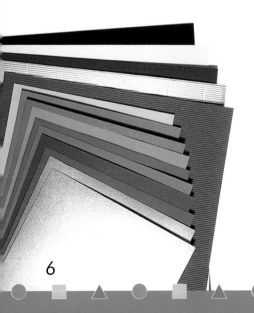

All sorts of *cardboard* and *paper* can be used for making handmade cards. Colored *posterboard* and construction paper are ideal and *corrugated* and *metallic cardboard* can be very effective.

Colored *pens* are used to draw and color designs. *Paint pens* and *metallic pens* are great because they show up on most colored backgrounds. You can also use *felt-tipped pens.* A *thin black pen* is used to outline designs.

It is safest to use a **blunt**-ended needle like a tapestry needle for sewing.

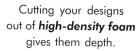

Plastic eyes create lively characters and add movement to cards. Beads are used for decoration and **polystyrene** balls are excellent for creating snow.

Cutting your designs out of **high-density foam** gives them depth.

Pencil lines are rubbed out with an eraser. A ruler is used for measuring and to draw and score straight lines.

Fantastic paint effects can be created with an old toothbrush and a sponge.

The paints used in this book are water-based. Acrylics, water colors, or poster paints are best.

Transparent tape holds sandwich bags and thread in place. Masking tape is used to secure a design when transferring it.

Fabrics such as felt are great for adding texture. Scissors are used for cutting paper, thread, fabric, and high-density foam. Use an old pair for cutting sandpaper.

Place thick **corrugated** cardboard under your card when piercing holes. Fine sandpaper can be used to add texture.

Colored and metallic thread is used for sewing and beading.

A glue stick is perfect for sticking paper and cardboard together. Strong, clear glue is used to stick fabric and decorations together.

Nazca Birds

In the 1930s, pilots were flying over the desert in Peru in South America when they saw giant drawings on the ground. There was a monkey the size of a soccer field, a lizard twice that length, a spider, fish, birds, and insects. It is thought that they were made by the Nazca Indians around two thousand years ago, but nobody knows why. Have a look at them in a library or on the Internet and try to imagine why they were made and how. This card is inspired by a Nazca drawing of a large bird called a condor.

YOU WILL NEED

Fine sandpaper
Corrugated cardboard
Empty ballpoint pen
Scissors • Ruler
Strong, clear glue
Paper • Glue stick

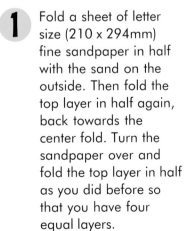

Ask an adult to help you photocopy the design.

2 Photocopy the design on page 30. Cut around it roughly and glue it to the folded sandpaper with a glue stick. Make sure that the dotted line that runs down one side of the pattern is up against one of the outer folds. Don't worry if the bird's wings overlap the edge.

1 Fold a sheet of letter size (210 x 294mm) fine sandpaper in half with the sand on the outside. Then fold the top layer in half again, back towards the center fold. Turn the sandpaper over and fold the top layer in half as you did before so that you have four equal layers.

3 Carefully cut out the bird shape. Make sure you do not cut off the ends of the feathers that have dotted lines. They should extend to meet the fold.

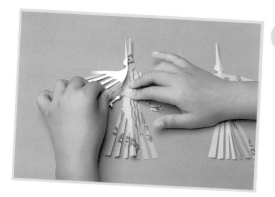

4 Unfold the sandpaper to reveal two condors joined at the wings. Peel off the photocopied pattern. Do not worry if some parts will not peel off—they will not show.

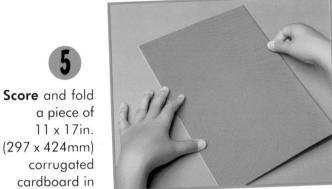

5

Score and fold a piece of 11 x 17in. (297 x 424mm) corrugated cardboard in half widthways to make a card (see page 28).

6 Glue the condors to the card with strong, clear glue.

FURTHER IDEAS
Invent your own fold-out Nazca style designs using geometric shapes, straight lines, and repeated patterns.

Fantasy Planets

Space . . . the final frontier! What is out there? We know about the planets in our own solar system, but we cannot be sure about what lies beyond. Many people are fascinated by space and all of the unanswered questions we have about the universe. Picturing outer space, you can let your imagination run wild! In this project, spattering white paint on black posterboard makes the perfect starry background for your own fantasy solar system. You can create all kinds of weird and wonderful planets using paints and metallic pens.

YOU WILL NEED
Black posterboard
Colored paper • Paints
Metallic pens • Pencil
Empty ballpoint pen • Ruler
Sponge • Toothbrush
Scissors • Compass
Glue

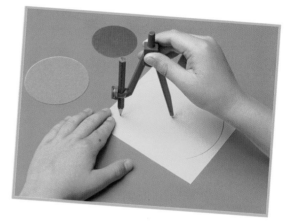

1 **Score** and fold a piece of black posterboard in half. Dip the end of a toothbrush in some white paint and slowly run your finger over the bristles so that the paint spatters onto the posterboard. Allow the paint to dry. You can spatter on a second color if you like.

Note Practice spattering and sponging on scrap paper first, and always cover your work surface.

2 To make the planets, use a compass to draw four different-sized circles on colored paper. Cut them out.

3

Put one of the circles on some newspaper. Dip a sponge in paint and lightly stroke the color half way across from one side. Stroking in a slight curve will make the planet look **three-dimensional**.

4

Sponge another color across from the other side and then spatter more colors over the top with the toothbrush. Experiment with sponging, spattering, and using metallic pens to decorate the other planets. Let the paint dry.

5

Using the pattern on page 29 as a guide, draw a planet ring on paper. Make sure it will fit over one of your planets. Then cut it out and lightly sponge some paint across it. Let the paint dry.

6

Slip the ring over a planet. Move the planets around on your space background until you are happy with the picture. Then glue them all in place.

FURTHER IDEAS

Add aliens, rockets, **meteors**, or space ships to your fantasy solar system.

Matisse Collage

Henri Matisse was a famous French artist. He was influenced by many different styles. Once when Matisse was ill, he found it difficult to paint, so he made pictures by cutting shapes out of paper and gluing them down to make a collage. "I am drawing directly in color," he said.

In this project you will learn how to make a collage inspired by Matisse. There is a pattern on page 30 to help you, but if you feel confident, try cutting out your own picture **freehand** as Matisse did.

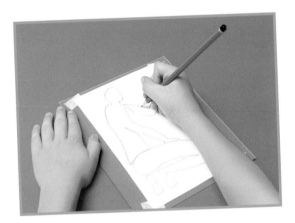

1 **Transfer** the pattern on page 30 onto colored paper, or draw it freehand if you prefer.

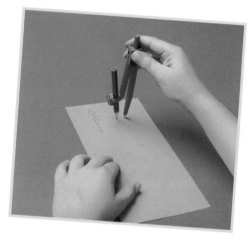

2 On a different colored piece of construction paper, draw or transfer the plant design. Then, using a compass, draw a circle roughly 1in. (25mm) across.

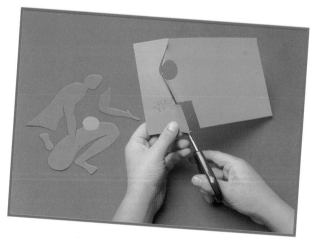

3 Cut out all of the shapes using scissors.

12

4 Take an 8½ x 5½in. (210 x 148mm) piece of construction paper and trim about ¼in. (6mm) off each side. Try to leave an uneven edge as you cut.

5 Arrange the pieces on the paper, leaving small gaps in the figure as shown. Glue them in place with a glue stick.

6 **Score** and fold a piece of letter size (210 x 294mm) posterboard in half and glue the finished collage to the front.

FURTHER IDEAS
Cut out the shapes for figures, animals, or plants to make your own original collages.

It's a Goal!

Soccer is a great game to play and to watch. Its history dates as far back as the ancient Chinese, Greek, **Mayan**, and Egyptian societies. Modern soccer developed from games played in England in the nineteenth century. In 1863, these games were separated into rugby, which is where football comes from, and Association football, or soccer. You can make this soccer goal card by sewing the net with colored thread, attaching the goal posts, and finally putting the ball in the net—one to zero!

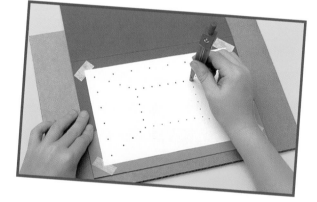

YOU WILL NEED
Posterboard • Construction paper
Strong, clear glue • Glue stick
Blunt-ended needle • Scissors
Masking tape • Pencil • Paper
Corrugated cardboard
Thick colored thread
Compass • Black pen

 Score and fold a piece of letter size (210 x 294mm) posterboard in half to make the card. Glue a strip of green construction paper across the bottom.

2 Photocopy the dot pattern on page 31 and secure it to the front of the card with masking tape. Open the card and lay the front over a piece of thick corrugated cardboard to protect your work surface. Using the point of your compass, pierce holes through the dots on the pattern. Then remove the pattern.

> **!** Ask an adult to help you photocopy the design.

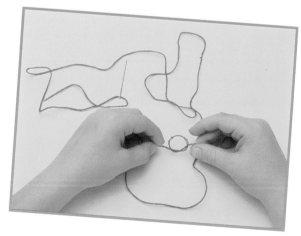

Thread one end of a long piece of colored thread through the eye of a blunt-ended needle. Tie a large knot in the other end.

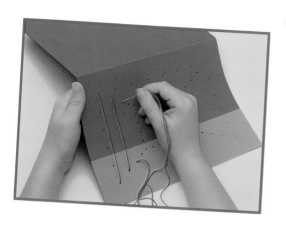

4

Push the needle up through the hole in the bottom left-hand corner and down through the hole in the top left-hand corner. Do the same for the next holes and continue until all the **vertical** lines are sewn.

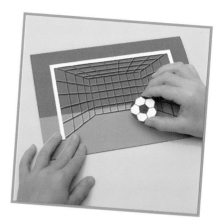

5

Now sew all the other lines of the net, as shown. You will use some holes more than once. If you run out of thread, tie a knot in the first thread and thread your needle again.

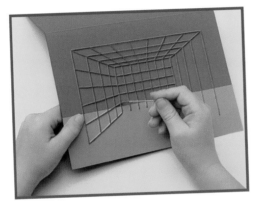

6

Transfer the goal posts and the soccer ball design on page 31 onto white construction paper and cut them out. Color the soccer ball with a black pen as shown. Use strong, clear glue to attach the goal posts and ball to the card.

FURTHER IDEAS
Sew a basketball hoop, tennis racket, spider's web, or even somebody's name to make an unusual card.

Spooky Woods

The woods can be very spooky at night. It is easy to imagine pairs of eyes peeping out from the dark. Woods and forests are often used to conjure up a spooky atmosphere in paintings, stories, poems, and movies. Collect interesting looking sticks and twigs to make the trees in this spooky woods card. Imagine the different creatures that live in the woods as you glue on their eyes. You could even write a spooky poem in the card.

YOU WILL NEED

Bright single **corrugated** cardboard
Posterboard • Empty ballpoint pen
Ruler • Scissors • Plastic eyes
Masking tape • Pencil • Paper
Sticks • Strong, clear glue
Black felt

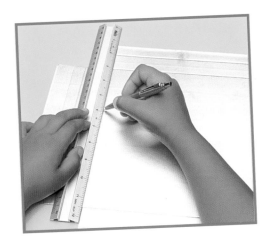

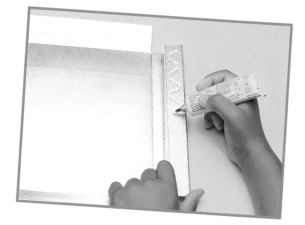

1 Enlarge the design on page 31 on a photocopier and **transfer** it onto the back of a piece of bright corrugated cardboard. Enlarge the design by 141% to fit on a sheet of letter size, or by 200%, to fit on a sheet of 11 x 17in. (244 x 297mm) paper. Cut it out, **score** and fold along the dotted lines.

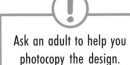

Ask an adult to help you photocopy the design.

2 Fold the left-hand side of the cardboard to make a rectangular tube. Squeeze a line of strong, clear glue onto the corrugated side of the end tab and stick it in place. Do the same on the right, but leave the top and bottom open.

3 Measure the flat area left in the middle. Cut out a piece of black felt the same size. Glue it to the cardboard with strong, clear glue.

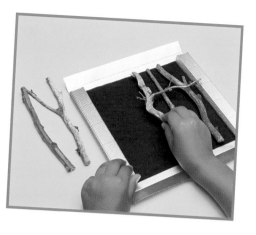

4 Trim the sticks so that they fit roughly inside the flat area. Then arrange them on top of the felt to look like woods.

!

Ask an adult to help you cut the sticks.

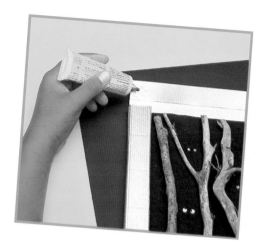

5

When you are happy with the picture, glue down the sticks with strong, clear glue. Then glue pairs of plastic eyes in between the sticks. Let the glue dry.

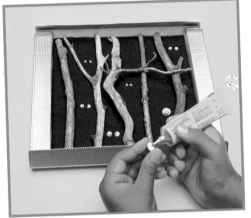

6

Finish the frame by gluing down the corners of the top and bottom flaps. Finally, glue the finished frame to a piece of folded posterboard.

FURTHER IDEAS
Spray sticks with snow spray or silver paint and add a silvery moon to make a winter scene.

Funky Fish

Fish are very beautiful. It is amazing how many different shapes and colors they can be. We have only explored one hundredth of the seabeds on our planet, so there may be even more weird and wonderful varieties of fish to be discovered in the future. In this project, fish shapes are threaded onto metallic thread with beads to make a bubbly underwater scene.

YOU WILL NEED

Posterboard • Construction paper
Metallic thread • Compass
Glue stick • Strong, clear glue
Transparent tape • Beads • Plastic eyes
Masking tape • Pencil
Empty ballpoint pen
Scissors

1 **Score** and fold a piece of posterboard in half. Using a compass, draw a circle overlapping the fold and the bottom by about ¼in. (6mm) as shown. Cut it out.

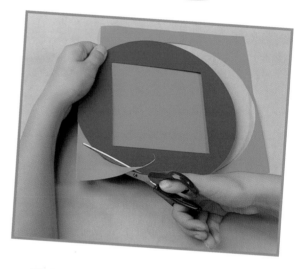

2 Open the circular card and draw a square on the front. Cut out the square to make a window. Glue a piece of construction paper on the inside back of the card (the side you can see through the window) and trim it so it fits.

3 Fold three small pieces of construction paper in half. **Transfer** one of the fish designs on page 29 onto each piece of paper. Cut out the fish—you will have two of each design.

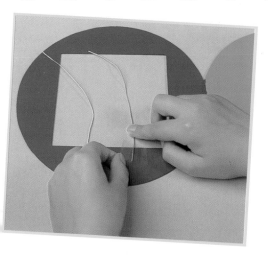

4

Lay two pieces of metallic thread over the window on the inside of the card. Secure them at the bottom with transparent tape.

5

Thread some beads onto the first piece of metallic thread. Then take a pair of fish and put glue on one of them. Press the fish together, sandwiching the thread between them as shown.

6

Thread on more beads and secure the top of the thread with tape. Do the same with the other thread, using more beads and the other two fish. Finally, glue plastic eyes on both sides of the fish using strong, clear glue.

FURTHER IDEAS

Make a card with a different-shaped window. Add other sea creatures—an octopus, seahorse, or dolphin.

Smiling Sunflower

Flowers are often used to cheer people up. People also give flowers on special occasions like Mother's Day and Valentine's Day. Different flowers can mean different things. Red flowers—roses, carnations, and tulips—are usually for love. White flowers, such as daisies and lilies, represent innocence. Pansies and poppies are for remembrance, sweet peas for goodbyes, and forget-me-nots speak for themselves! Sunflowers turn their heads to follow the sun across the sky. This one has a lovely smile and a stem made from flexible pipe cleaners, so that its head bobs cheerfully when it moves.

YOU WILL NEED

Posterboard • Pipe cleaners
Scissors • Ruler • Pen
Plastic eyes • Pencil
Masking tape • Paper
Compass • Eraser • Felt
Empty ballpoint pen
Strong, clear glue

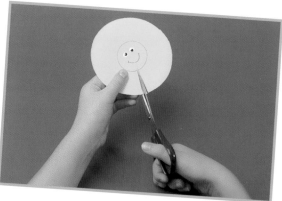

2 Cut a slit from the edge up to the small circle. Then cut a second slit next to it. Continue all of the way around the face. Carefully erase the pencil circle.

1 Use a compass and a pencil to draw a large circle on some yellow posterboard, and then cut it out. Lightly draw a smaller circle in the middle for the sunflower's face. Glue on plastic eyes using strong, clear glue. With a pen, draw a smile.

3 Fold every other petal away from you until there is a space between each one. Then hold all of the folded petals together and wrap the end of a pipe cleaner around them until they are secure. The rest of this pipe cleaner will be the sunflower's stem.

4

Twist more pipe cleaners around the stem to make it longer and thicker. Cut two sets of leaves out of felt. Push the leaves between the pipe cleaners as shown.

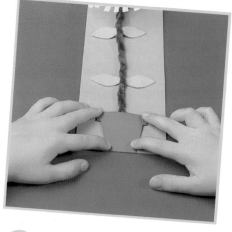

5

Transfer the pattern for the flowerpot on page 29 onto posterboard. Cut it out. **Score** along the dotted lines as shown and fold back the tabs.

6

Score and fold a piece of letter size (210 x 294mm) posterboard in half lengthways. Glue the bottom half of the flower stem to the card. Put glue on the flowerpot tabs and press the pot over the stem.

FURTHER IDEAS
Create flowers using textured papers or metallic posterboard. Try making several layers of petals.

Pop-up Dinosaur

Millions of years ago there were no people, and dinosaurs ruled the earth. We know from digging up their bones what kinds of dinosaurs existed, their sizes and shapes, and even what they ate. We do not know what colors they were, though, so when you make this pop-up dinosaur card, imagine the colors for yourself. Create a prehistoric world of your own. There are patterns for the Tyrannosaurus Rex and the Pteranodon in the back of the book, but you could draw any of your favorite dinosaurs—or even invent your own.

Score and fold a piece of posterboard in half. On the top half of the inside, sponge on a strip of paint to suggest a landscape. Let the paint dry.

Note Sponging two similar colors on top of each other can make a landscape look more realistic.

2 Transfer the Tyrannosaurus Rex and Pteranodon designs on page 30 onto posterboard. Color them using paint pens.

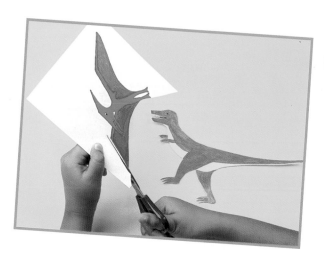

3 Draw the outlines and the eyes of the dinosaurs with a thin black pen. Carefully cut the dinosaurs out. If some areas are difficult to cut out, color them black so that they will not show up.

4

Decide where you want your dinosaur to stand, and mark the spot lightly with a pencil. Fold the card inside out. From the fold side, cut two slits up to the mark you have made.

5

Open up the card and press between the cuts to push out a tab. Then close the card again with the tab pushed out and press the tab into the right position.

6

Open the card and glue the Tyrannosaurus's leg to the tab with strong, clear glue. Glue the Pteranodon to the background.

Note To make the Pteranodon stand out from the card, stick a little pad of folded posterboard on the back before gluing it in place.

FURTHER IDEAS
Make pop-up scenery for your dinosaur world: hills, trees, plants, mountains—even a volcano!

Jazzy Guitar

Guitars are played all over the world to make all kinds of music — from Spanish **flamenco** and folk music to pop, rock, and jazz. Guitars usually have six strings, although there are twelve-string guitars too. Each string plays a different note depending on how **taut** it is. Strings can be adjusted to the right **pitch** using a special tuning key. You can make a card in the shape of a guitar and add strings made from colored thread.

YOU WILL NEED

Posterboard • Scissors
Glue stick • Pencil • Paper
Masking tape • Compass
Colored thread • **Blunt**-ended needle
Corrugated cardboard
Paint pens

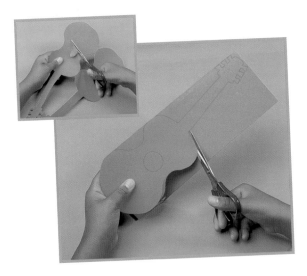

1 Score and fold a piece of colored posterboard in half and **transfer** the outer guitar design on page 29 onto it. Make sure that the dotted edges marked on the pattern go over the fold line. Cut out the guitar. Open the card and cut out the circle in the middle from the front of the card only.

2 Transfer the inner guitar pattern and the neck and soundboard patterns onto colored posterboard and cut them out.

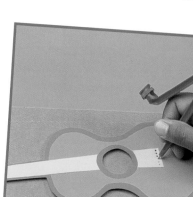

3 Glue the inner guitar, neck, and soundboard to the card. Open the card and lay it on some thick corrugated cardboard. Pierce the sets of holes on the neck and the soundboard with a compass.

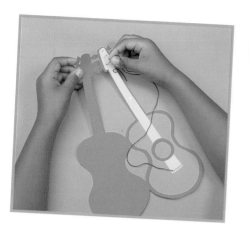

4 Thread one end of a piece of colored thread through the eye of a blunt-ended needle and tie a knot in the other end. Sew up through the far left hole at the bottom and down through the far left hole at the top.

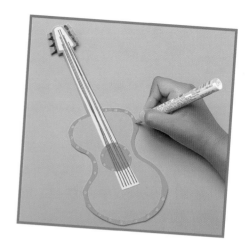

5

Gently pull the thread through until it is taut. Do not pull it too tight, or the card will bend. Wrap the end around the bottom left tuning key and tie a knot. Repeat for the other five strings.

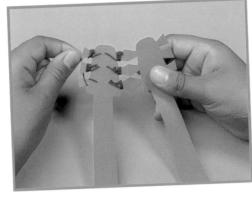

6 Decorate your guitar by drawing big dots around the edge with a paint pen.

Note If you find knotting the thread difficult, you can tape the loose ends to the back.

FURTHER IDEAS

Try making other musical instruments. A banjo has five strings, a double bass has four, and a harp has lots and lots.

Winter Window

Many cultures around the world have a winter festival. Most of them are linked to the winter solstice. The solstice marks the shortest day and longest night of the year. Some of the festivals celebrated during winter are Christmas, Kwanzaa, Hanukkah, and Yule. Winter is a lovely time to gather with family and friends and stay warm by the fire. You can make a winter window card using polystyrene balls for snow and a clear plastic bag, such as a sandwich or freezer bag, for the window.

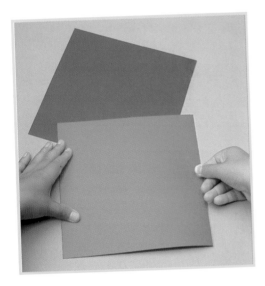

Cut out two pieces of posterboard, one 16½ x 8¼in. (42 x 21cm), and one 8¼in. (21cm) square. Fold the big one in half.

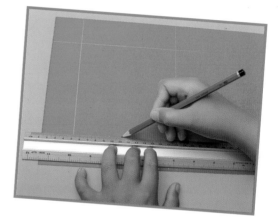

2 On the inside front of the folded card, measure 1½in. (4cm) in from each side and draw lines to make a square. Cut out the square.

3 Open up the card again and lay a clear sandwich bag over the square. You may need to trim the top of the bag to fit. Tape it at the bottom and sides. Do not stretch the bag too tightly, or the card will warp.

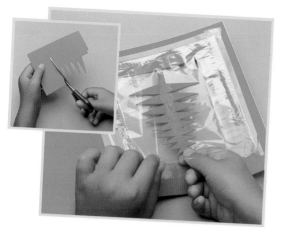

 4

Draw a tree on high-density foam and cut it out. Put a line of glue down the middle of the tree and press it inside the bag. Make sure the glued side of the tree is up.

 5

Sprinkle some polystyrene balls into the bag and tape the top shut.

 6

Spread strong, clear glue on the inside of the card window frame. Press the square piece of posterboard against the back of the window.

FURTHER IDEAS

You can make all sorts of things to stand in your snow storm—try a snowman, a house, a reindeer, or a penguin.

Techniques

Transferring a design

You can photocopy the patterns on pages 29–31 and transfer them onto paper using the technique shown below. Use the photocopier to enlarge or reduce the designs if you need to.

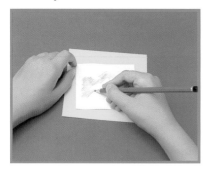 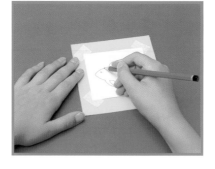 

1 Photocopy the design. Turn over the photocopy and scribble over the lines with a soft pencil.

2 Turn over the photocopy and tape it to your card using masking tape. Then go over the lines of the design with a pencil.

3 Peel back the photocopy to reveal the transferred design.

Scoring and folding card

Dotted lines on the patterns need to be scored and folded. You can also use scoring to help make neat cards. Find the center line by measuring the halfway point, then score and fold as shown below.

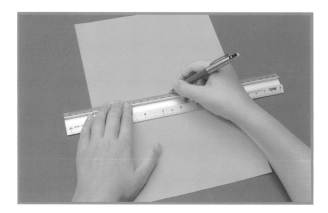 

1 Score a line across the middle of the card with a ballpoint pen that has run out of ink.

2 Fold the card and run the back of your fingernail along the fold to press it down. If the edges are not exactly square, you can trim them with scissors.

Patterns

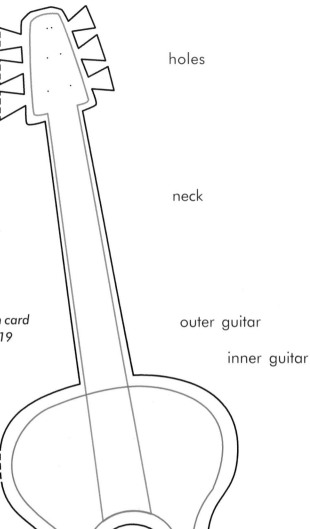

holes

neck

outer guitar

inner guitar

soundboard

holes

Patterns for the Funky Fish card
featured on pages 18–19

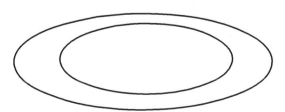

Pattern for the flowerpot in the Smiling
Sunflower card featured on pages 20–21

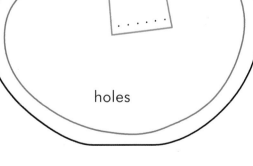

Pattern for the planet ring used in the Fantasy
Planets card featured on pages 10–11

Pattern for the Jazzy Guitar card featured
on pages 24–25

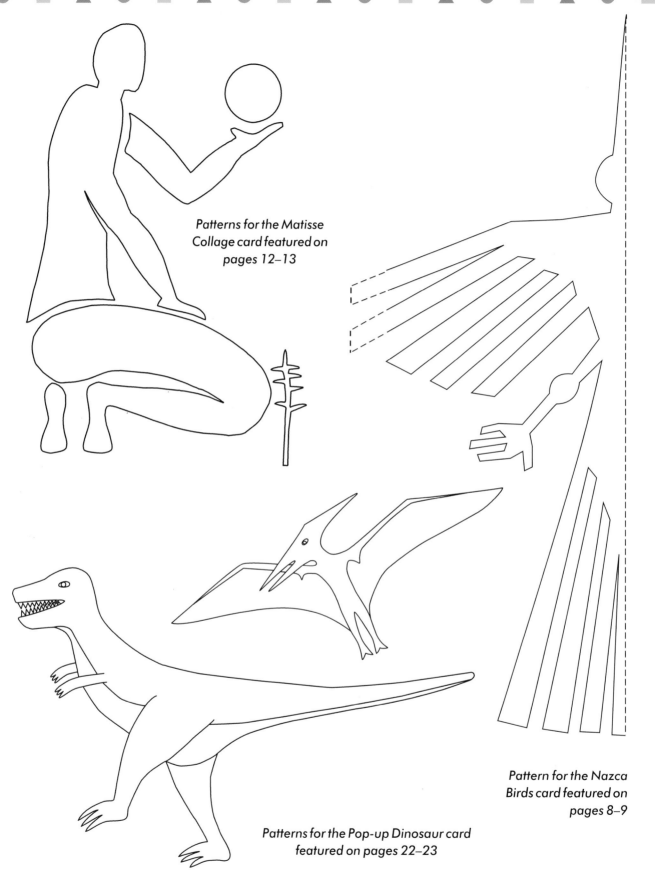

Patterns for the Matisse Collage card featured on pages 12–13

Patterns for the Pop-up Dinosaur card featured on pages 22–23

Pattern for the Nazca Birds card featured on pages 8–9

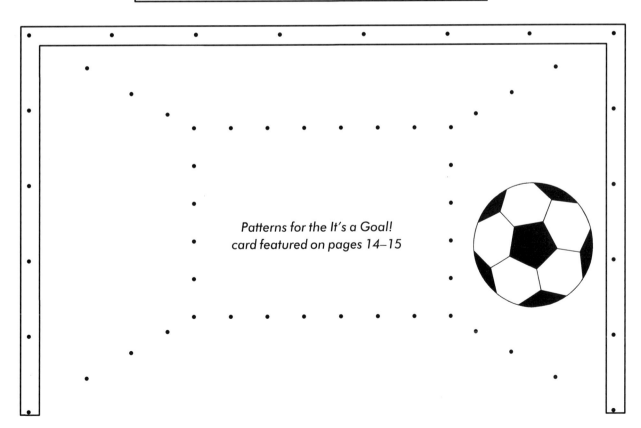

Pattern for the frame of the Spooky Woods card featured on pages 16–17

Patterns for the It's a Goal! card featured on pages 14–15

Glossary

Blunt   not sharp; something with a dull or rounded point

Corrugated   having a layer of ridges or grooves, often between two flat surfaces

Flamenco   a style of music from Spain that has a strong beat

Freehand   drawn by hand without the help of a pattern

High-density foam   special kind of foam used in arts and crafts that is sold at craft stores

Mayan   group of people who lived in the ninth century in what is now Central America

Meteor   a large burning boulder that travels through space; a shooting star

Pitch   musical key, or tone

Polystyrene   stiff, plastic foam often used for cups for hot liquids such as coffee and hot chocolate

Score   to carve or press lines and patterns into the surface of something

Taut   pulled tightly

Three-dimensional   seeming to have width, height, and depth; appearing real and solid

Transfer   to move something from one place to another

Transparent   see-through

Vertical   upright; straight up and down

Victorian   time in British history and arts from 1832 to 1901

More Books to Read

Devonshire, Hilary. *Greeting Cards and Gift Wrap.* New York : Franklin Watts, 1992.

Otten, Jack. *Watch Me Make a Birthday Card.* Danbury, Conn. : Children's Press, 2002.

Sogall, Kim. *Make Cards!* Cincinnati, Ohio : North Light Books, 1992.

Stowell, Charlotte. *Making Cards.* New York : Kingfisher, 1995.

Index